Adventures #3 ✝ with the Saints

Saint John Bosco
The Juggling Saint

Written by Maria Riley

Illustrated by Emily Mae

Rooted River Press

For my godson, Reid.
Grow in faith and have fun doing it!

www.mariarileyauthor.com

ISBN 978-1-959607-03-8

Printed in the United States of America

Adventures ✝ with the Saints

This book belongs to future

Saint _____.

Contents

Prologue: Meet the Martins   7

1.   Back to School   10

2.   The Last Day of Summer   19

3.   New School Jitters   28

4.   The Juggling Saint   38

5.   A Rope and a Shepherd   47

6.   The Gray Dog   56

7.   Back Home Again   65

8.   The First Day of School   73

About Saint John Bosco   81

Prologue
Meet the Martins

On the outside, the Martins look like an average family. They haven't always been that way. The Martins are an extra-special family.

There are three kids in the Martin family. This fall, Luke will be starting 5th grade, Becca will be starting 3rd grade, and Joshua will be starting 2nd grade. It is almost time for the new school year!

At the beginning of summer, there were only two kids in the Martin family. Becca was Mom and Dad's only biological child. Luke had been adopted a long time ago. Then this summer, they met Joshua.

He lived with them as a foster child. Mom and Dad just finalized the adoption a few weeks ago. That made Joshua the real and forever child of Mom and Dad. It also made Luke and Becca his real and forever brother and sister.

The fact that Luke and Joshua were adopted wasn't what made them extra special, though. One day, while spending time together in Luke and Joshua's bedroom, something amazing happened.

The three kids were sharing special items from their biological families. Joshua had a cross necklace that is the only thing he owns from his birth mom. Luke had a baptismal candle from his birth family. Becca had her special Bible given to her by Mom and Dad.

When the three children brought their special items together, Saint Rafael and their guardian angels took them on an amazing journey back to the time of Jesus' birth! They met Saint Joseph, who was holding and adoring Baby Jesus.

Then, a few weeks later, the three kids were taken on another amazing journey. Saint Rafael and their guardian angels took them to a convent to meet Saint Thérèse. She taught them all about the Little Way.

Now, another adventure awaits them. . .

Chapter 1
Back to School

Joshua stood between Luke and Becca. He faced the altar as the priest spoke.

"May God bless you," Father Rich said, "in the name of the Father, and of the Son, and of the Holy Spirit."

"Amen," said Joshua and everyone else at Mass.

"The Mass is ended. Now go forth in peace, to love and serve God and one another," said Father Rich with a big smile.

"Thanks be to God!" replied everyone in the church.

The piano started a joyful tune. The choir began the final song, and the whole congregation sang along.

The Martin family stayed in church for a few minutes while Mom and Dad said hello to some friends. Luke also went to say hi to a friend from school. Becca and Joshua stayed close to their parents.

Becca bounced on her toes. "Can we go? Please?" she asked Mom eagerly.

Mom smiled down at Becca. "Just a minute," she told her.

Joshua watched Becca. She was so excited, but he wasn't.

"Ok, let's go," Mom finally said, taking Dad's hand and walking to the parking lot. Luke, Becca, and Joshua got into the minivan and buckled their seat belts.

"It's a big day," Dad said. "Back-to-school shopping!"

"Yay!" squealed Becca. She couldn't wait.

"Sweet," said Luke. Even he was excited.

"We're gonna go home to get changed into comfy clothes and have lunch," Mom told them. "Then we'll go to the store."

By the time Joshua and Luke were dressed, Mom had everything for sandwiches on the table. Everyone made their own sandwich just the way they liked. Too soon for Joshua, it was time to leave.

Joshua wanted to be excited about back-to-school shopping, but all he could think about was starting at a new school in a few days. He didn't know anyone. He didn't have any friends. What if he didn't fit in? What if he got lost?

In no time, they arrived at the store. Mom wanted to shop for a new outfit and a pair of shoes for each child. Becca wanted to go with Mom.

Dad said, "That means us guys are headed this way." Dad took out the list of supplies from the school.

It didn't take long for Joshua to get distracted. Instead of worrying about school, he focused on finding the right color folders and notebooks. They found No. 2 pencils, colored pencils, and crayons. Luke found the skinny and fat markers. Dad spied the erasers and sticky notes on the top shelf. Joshua hunted for one more purple folder.

"Okay," said Dad. "Looks like we found everything on the list."

Joshua looked at their shopping cart. They sure had a lot of supplies!

"Only one thing left," said Luke.

"That's right," said Dad. "Let's go find the backpacks."

The three Martin men found the aisle with backpacks. Joshua couldn't believe how many different types and colors there were. They had black ones, rainbow ones, and sparkly ones. Some had a matching lunchbox. Others had more zippers and pockets than Joshua could count.

Dad found a purple one with a big butterfly on it. "I think Becca will like this one," he said.

Luke and Joshua nodded. Becca loved butterflies. She would love this backpack.

Luke found a black one with lots of zippers. It was very mature looking.

Joshua picked out a simple blue one. Blue was his favorite color. Even though it wasn't fancy, it had everything he needed. He loved it.

Dad, Luke, and Joshua walked to meet Mom and Becca.

"Look at this backpack Dad found for you," Joshua told Becca.

She smiled from ear to ear and jumped up and down hugging it. "I love it! I love it!" she yelled happily.

Mom held out two pairs of shoes. "What do you boys think about these?" she asked.

Joshua noticed that the sneakers Mom picked out for him

had blue on them. "Thanks Mom," he told her. "They're perfect."

Then Mom grabbed a pair of shorts and a shirt. "I picked these out for you, Joshua," she said. She held the other pair of shorts and shirt for Luke to see.

Both boys smiled and agreed. Mom was happy they liked the outfits. The truth was, they were just happy they didn't have to try anything on.

"Looks like that's everything then," Mom told them. "Time to head back home."

After they paid for everything, they walked back to the car.

"I can't wait to see who's in my class," Becca said. "I can't wait to meet my teacher and wear my new outfit. Thanks again, Mom and Dad!"

"Yes, thank you for all the supplies," said Joshua. He felt so blessed to be starting school with everything he needed.

"Yeah, thanks," said Luke.

"It's our pleasure," said Dad. "We are so proud of each of you. This is going to be a great school year. I just know it!"

Just like that, the dread returned to Joshua. As he thought about school, he became worried again. He wanted to believe Dad, but he just wasn't sure. Would it actually be a great school year?

Chapter 2
The Last Day of Summer

The door to the boys' bedroom creaked open.

A quiet voice started singing. "Oh, rise and shine, and give God your glory, glory."

Mom kept singing in the darkness. Joshua and Luke didn't stir. It was too early to get out of bed!

"Rise and shine and give God your glory, glory, children of the Lord," Mom sang, now at full volume.

"It's too early, Mom," groaned Luke.

"This is the time you'll be getting up for school starting tomorrow," she explained.

"But it's not school *today*," Luke said.

"I know," said Mom, "but we've got to start getting you used to waking up at this time."

Mom went to wake Becca and turned the boys' light on as she left.

Luke sat up on the top bunk. His legs dangled off the side, and Joshua could see the bottoms of his feet.

"I can't believe it's the last day of summer already," Joshua told Luke. The nerves in his belly started again.

"I know!" Luke replied. "This summer went by extra fast."

Joshua and Luke got dressed and went to have breakfast. They each poured a bowl of cereal. Becca joined them, still in her pajamas.

"It's too early," she yawned. She poured her own bowl of cereal.

It was funny seeing Becca so sleepy. She was almost always smiling, bouncing, and full of energy.

Dad walked into the kitchen dressed for work. "It's nice to see you three before I head to the office," he said. Most summer days, Dad was up and at the office before the kids woke up. They didn't get to see Dad until he came home.

"I do like seeing you," said Becca, "but I'd still rather be in bed."

Everyone laughed. Joshua secretly wished he was still in bed too.

After they said goodbye to Dad, Mom and the kids spread all the school supplies out on the kitchen table. Mom grabbed the supply lists from school and started passing them out.

This year, Luke had some different supplies. He had a three-ring binder and subject dividers for it. He was going to be changing classes for the first time.

Mom passed out the folders, crayons, and markers to Joshua and Becca. Luke got a ruler, a pack of notecards, and extra notebook paper. Everyone received pencils, erasers, and notebooks.

Becca, Luke, and Joshua carefully loaded the supplies into their backpacks. They zipped them up and put them by the front door for the next day.

Then they packed their lunches. Joshua carefully spread the mayo onto two pieces of bread. Then he layered a slice of turkey and a slice of cheese. He put that in his lunchbox along with some Goldfish, a piece of string cheese, a mandarin orange, and a bottle of water. He closed the lunchbox and put it in the fridge next to Luke's and Becca's lunches.

The rest of the day the kids spent reading, playing games, and swinging on the tire swing. They tried to pack in as much fun as they could.

The sun was still high in the sky when Dad arrived home. He went upstairs to change out of his work clothes. When he came down, he was wearing his bathing suit.

"Are we going to the pool?" asked Becca.

"Go put on your bathing suits and meet me outside," Dad said with a smile on his face.

The three kids ran to get their bathing suits on. Dad and Mom were in the backyard standing next to a big cooler. They opened the cooler and reached in. Mom and Dad had a water balloon in each hand.

Mom and Dad laughed and threw the water balloons at their children.

"Gotcha!" yelled Dad, as a water balloon exploded on Becca.

"Water balloon fight!" yelled the three kids.

Luke, Becca, and Joshua ran to the cooler and grabbed some water balloons. All five members of the Martin family ran around throwing water balloons and getting wet.

Becca laughed as she threw a water balloon at Mom. Mom jumped out of the way, and it exploded on Dad.

Luke and Joshua threw water balloons at each other. Water balloons were flying in every direction!

After a while they ran out of balloons. They all were breathing heavily from running around.

"That was awesome!" said Becca.
"It was Dad's idea," said Mom.

"Thanks, Dad," said Joshua.

"Okay, time to clean up," announced Dad.

Everyone walked around the yard picking up pieces of the balloons. Joshua noticed that the red and yellow balloon pieces were easy to find. Some of the green pieces were hard to find. They blended in with the green grass.

"Time to get dressed," Mom told the kids. "I'm going to start dinner."

"Thanks again, Dad," said Luke as they walked inside.

"You're welcome," replied Dad. "I really wanted to make your last day of summer extra special."

Joshua was grateful that Dad had such a fun idea. He just really wished summer never had to end.

Chapter 3
New School Jitters

The Martin family sat down for dinner. Mom made hot dogs, homemade macaroni and cheese, and fresh green beans. Before anyone took a bite, they said grace.

They all prayed together: "In the name of the Father, and of the Son, and of the Holy Spirit. Amen. Bless us, O Lord, and these Thy gifts, which we are about to receive, from Thy bounty, through Christ, our Lord. Amen."

"Delicious dinner," said Becca. She immediately took a big bite of the macaroni and cheese. "Your macaroni and cheese is the best!"

"Yes, thank you," said Luke and Joshua.

Dad said, "Let's all talk about what we're most excited about for the new school year."

Mom started, "I'm excited for you kids to make some new friends. Plus, I'm looking forward to having time to volunteer more at church."

Dad went next, "I'm excited about all the things you are going to learn this year."

"For me," said Luke, "I'm excited about switching classes. Plus, we're the oldest in the school."

Mom and Dad smiled and nodded. Mom said, "I can't believe this is your last year in elementary school. You are growing up so fast!" She wiped a tear out of her eye.

Becca shared next. "I'm excited to see my old friends and make some new ones."

Joshua wasn't surprised that Becca was excited about friends. She loved to play with other kids at the park and pool. Joshua didn't make friends as easily as Becca did. That worried him.

"What about you, Joshua?" Mom asked. "What are you looking forward to?"

"Um," Joshua said, "I guess meeting my new teacher."

"Ms. Harken is the best," said Becca. "That's who I had last year."

Joshua just shrugged. He didn't know Ms. Harken. He didn't know any of the teachers. He didn't know anything about this new school. It was scary to think about.

After dinner, Dad decided to do the dishes by himself. This was another treat for the last day of summer. Usually, the kids helped clean up after dinner.

Luke and Joshua went to their bedroom. They each took out their new shirt and shorts and laid them on the floor. Then they put a pair of socks on the outfit. They were all set for the morning.

Joshua kept feeling more nervous about school. He didn't think he would have a good day since he wouldn't know anyone in the 2nd grade.

"What's wrong?" asked Luke.

"I'm scared about starting a new school," replied Joshua.

"It's a great school," said Luke. "Everyone is really nice. You're gonna love it."

"That's easy for you to say," said Joshua. "You know a lot of people there."

"You're gonna fit right in," Luke said.

"What if I don't?" asked Joshua. He rubbed his cross necklace. It was the only thing he had from his biological mom. He always rubbed it when he was nervous.

"Hmmmm," said Luke. "I don't know. I just believe that it will be great."

"How do you believe that if you don't know it for sure?" asked Joshua.

Becca stepped into their room. "Believe what?" she asked.

"Joshua is nervous about the first day of school," Luke said.

"It's gonna be great!" said Becca.

"How do you know?" asked Joshua. They seemed so sure. He didn't feel sure at all.

"I don't know," said Becca. "But I just know."

Joshua sat down, feeling worse. His stomach flipped, and he did not want to go to school tomorrow. He felt awful.

Joshua kept rubbing his thumb on his cross necklace. The necklace started to feel warm.

Joshua knew what that meant. It meant Rafael the Archangel was preparing to take them on another adventure!

Joshua pulled out the glowing cross necklace. Luke and Becca knew exactly what to do. Luke took his baptismal candle from his dresser. Becca ran to her room to get her Bible.

All three items began to glow with a bright light. Beautiful white rays of light streamed in all directions from all three items.

Becca placed her Bible on the floor. It opened to the 10th chapter of the Gospel according to John.

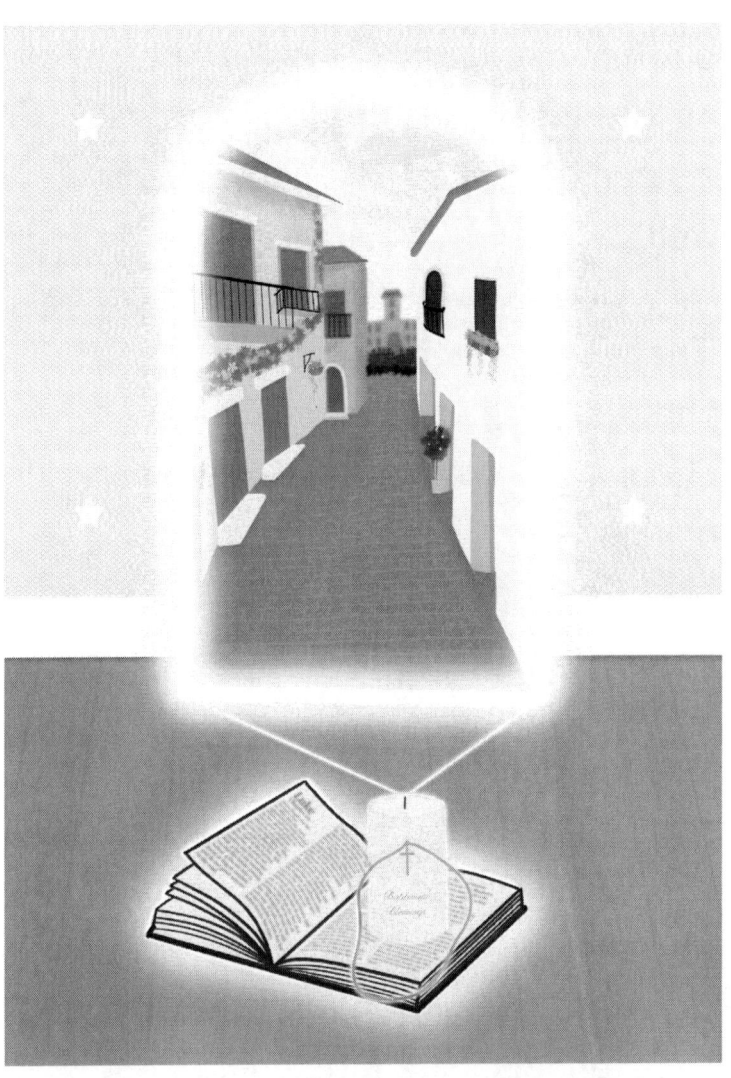

Joshua carefully placed his cross
into the indentation on Luke's

baptismal candle. Luke put the candle on the Bible, and the giant movie screen appeared on the bedroom wall.

Joshua walked up to the scene. There was a cobblestone road. In the distance, a large crowd was cheering. It looked like they were having fun.

Joshua stepped onto the street. Becca and Luke followed him. They turned around, but the bedroom had already disappeared. Instead, they saw Saint Rafael hovering there.

"Hello, kids," the angel said warmly.

"Hi!" said the kids to Rafael and their angels. The kids couldn't see their guardian angels. But they knew their angels were always there.

"Where are we?" asked Becca.

Rafael replied, "This is Turin, a town in Italy. There's someone special over there in the crowd."

"I think we know what to do this time," said Luke. "Thanks, Rafael!"

"My pleasure," said the angel as he faded from their sight.

Chapter 4
The Juggling Saint

The children waved goodbye to Saint Rafael. They walked toward the crowd. They heard laughing and cheering as they got closer.

Most of the people in the crowd were boys about Luke's age or a little older. It wasn't hard to see what they were cheering about. A man walked slowly across a rope tied between two trees. He was walking on a homemade tightrope!

Joshua felt nervous watching him and said, "I hope he doesn't fall."

"I bet he does this all the time," said Becca.

The man stopped halfway across the rope. It seemed like he might lose his balance. His body swayed a little bit. A big gasp sounded from the crowd. Slowly, the man turned around. He walked the rest of the way backward!

He jumped off at the end. The crowd cheered loudly. The man smiled warmly and bowed.

"Would you like to see more?" he asked.

"Yes!" the crowd yelled back.

The friendly man picked up a red apple off the ground. He tossed it into the air. Then he picked up two more. In no time, he was juggling three apples.

"Another!" the man yelled. A boy nearby tossed him another apple.

Now he was juggling four. The crowd cheered louder.

"And another!" the man yelled again. The boy tossed a fifth apple. The kids couldn't believe he was juggling five apples at the same time.

The man stopped and caught the apples. One, two, three, four, five. Becca, Luke, and Joshua joined the cheering.

"For my next act," said the man, "I'll need a little space." The crowd of children spread out. They made a big circle with the man standing in the middle.

Luke turned to a boy next to him. "Who is that man?" he asked.

"That's Father John Bosco," the boy said. "We call him Don Bosco. Don means father in Italian."

"That's a priest?" asked Becca.

"Yes," said the boy. "He's the best priest I've ever met!"

Wow," said Joshua. "I didn't know priests could juggle or walk on tightropes!"

"I've never met a priest like this," said Luke. Becca and Joshua nodded. They had never seen Father Rich juggle in Mass before. And Father Rich definitely never walked on a tightrope.

Father John Bosco yelled, "Watch out!" He did three front walkovers in a row.

"Wow," said Becca. "He can even do gymnastics."

"I've only seen stuff like this on TV," said Luke.

It was exciting to see this in person. Father John Bosco had many talents.

Then he did a handstand in the middle of the circle. He didn't fall down. He walked on his hands all the way around the crowd.

"Wow!" said Joshua. He was amazed by what this priest could do.

"That is awesome!" added Becca.

The crowd cheered loudly. Becca, Joshua, and Luke clapped and cheered too.

The audience crowded around the priest again. He started walking around the group.

He came close to where the kids were standing. "What's this in your nose?" Don Bosco asked Luke.

Luke looked puzzled. Did he have a big booger stuck in his nose?

The priest smiled and reached toward Luke's nose. "Aha!" he said. "You had this nut in there."

Everyone laughed as Don Bosco pulled a small nut from Luke's nose. Then he popped it into his mouth! Joshua and Becca laughed.

Don Bosco continued to walk around the crowd. "What do you have in your pocket?" he asked another boy.

"What?" asked the boy. He looked confused. He slowly pulled something out of his pocket.

"A watch!" said the priest.

"Hey," said a different boy. "That's my watch!"

The crowd burst into laughter again. Don Bosco returned the watch to its owner. He continued to walk around making nuts come out of noses and ears. He made watches and necklaces appear in pockets.

The children all watched and cheered as the priest performed magic tricks.

All the boys who were watching the priest seemed to be having a good time. It was a great show!

Joshua, Becca, and Luke had never been to a street performance before. It was fun. Don Bosco knew most of the children. He called many of them by name.

"It's time for the great finale," said Don Bosco. "Everyone, come close. Squeeze in, so everyone can hear."

All of the children gathered around the priest. Joshua wondered what he was going to finish with.

Chapter 5
A Rope and a Shepherd

"This," Don Bosco said, "is the most important trick of all." He pulled out three pieces of rope. He held them up one at a time. He showed everyone that they were three separate pieces of rope.

"Watch closely," the priest said. He took the three pieces of rope and rolled them into a ball. He waved one hand over the other.

Don Bosco picked up one end of a rope. He lifted it into the air and all three pieces had become one long rope! There wasn't a single knot.

"How did he do that?" asked Joshua.

"I don't know," said Luke. "I was watching him the whole time."

"He's a great magician," said Becca.

Don Bosco spoke to the crowd. "You see, this rope is more than just a rope. This rope helps us to understand God."

"Huh?" said some of the boys watching. Luke, Becca, and Joshua also felt confused. How could a rope help them understand God?

"God is three persons in one," said the priest. Just like that, the rope was in three pieces again.

He held up the first piece of the rope. "The first person of the Holy Trinity is God the Father." Then Don Bosco held up the second piece of the rope. He said, "The second person of the Holy Trinity is God the Son, who is Jesus."

Many of the boys in the crowd were nodding. They had heard about Jesus.

Luke called out, "The last one is the Holy Spirit!"

"That's right, young man!" said Don Bosco. He smiled proudly at Luke. He picked up the third piece of rope. He said, "The last person of the Holy Trinity is God the Holy Spirit."

He continued, "They are all three separate, and yet all one God."

"How can that be?" asked a boy. "How can they be different and the same?"

The priest smiled. "Great question! The answer is in the rope." He waved his hand over the rope, and it became one long rope again.

"It is just like how this one long rope is made up of three different ropes. Our God is made up of three different persons. God the Father, God the Son, and God the Holy Spirit."

"Now," said Don Bosco, "who remembers the Gospel reading from this week?"

The crowd went silent. One hand went up in the middle of the group.

"Yes, Marco?" asked Don Bosco.

"Jesus is the Good Shepherd," said Marco.

"Excellent!" replied the priest. "We are His sheep, and Jesus is our shepherd."

"What exactly does that mean?" called out one boy from the crowd.

Don Bosco smiled at the boy. "What is the job of a shepherd?"

"To watch over the sheep," said one boy.

"To keep them safe from wolves," said another boy.

"To make sure they don't get lost," said another boy.

"That's right!" said Don Bosco. "So that's what Jesus is saying when He tells us that He is the Good Shepherd. It means that Jesus loves us. He watches over us. He protects us."

Don Bosco continued, "In fact, a good shepherd will even sacrifice his own life to keep the sheep safe."

"Jesus did that for us on the cross!" yelled Becca.

"Exactly!" replied Don Bosco. "And that is why Jesus is our Good Shepherd."

"This is the best school I've ever been in," said Luke.

"I wish learning was always this fun," said Becca.

All of a sudden, Joshua felt a funny feeling in his stomach. Talking about school reminded him that he had to start at a new school tomorrow. He felt nervous anytime he thought about it.

Each boy in the crowd was listening to Don Bosco. They nodded their heads as they learned about Jesus the Good Shepherd.

"Now," said Don Bosco, "it's almost time for me to leave."

"Awww," said the crowd. They didn't want the show to be over.

"I have one last request before I go," he said. "Please bring me a pebble."

Everyone in the crowd bent down to pick up a pebble. They lined up to hand their pebble to Don Bosco.

"This is a remarkable pebble," the priest said to the first boy. He rolled the pebble between his fingers. When he handed it back to the boy, it had turned into a piece of candy!

One at a time, the boys handed a pebble to Don Bosco. He would then shake it, blow on it, or squeeze it. Each time, he turned it into candy.

He then handed the candy to the boy.

"May God bless you and keep you," Don Bosco told each boy.

"Thank you, Father," they said in return. Then they walked away with a smile on their face and candy in their mouth.

One by one, the crowd got smaller. Joshua, Luke, and Becca started to feel nervous. There weren't many kids left. Don Bosco was turning the last boy's pebble into a piece of candy.

The boy said goodbye and walked away. Now the three children stood there alone with the juggling priest.

Chapter 6
The Gray Dog

"Hello, children," said Don Bosco to Joshua, Luke, and Becca. "It's about time to go home."

Since Luke was the oldest, he took the lead. "We were hoping we could talk to you."

The street circus was a lot of fun, but they hadn't learned their lesson yet. Luke knew they needed to talk more to Don Bosco.

"How about you walk home with me?" said the priest.

The three children nodded and started walking next to him.

"I haven't seen you three before," said the priest.

"We're new," said Becca. "I'm Becca, and these are my brothers, Luke and Joshua."

"Welcome," he said. "What brings you to the city of Turin?"

The kids exchanged a look. Joshua said, "You. We wanted to talk to you."

"Excellent. What did you want to talk about?" he asked them.

"Well . . ." said Becca. She wasn't exactly sure what to say.

"Ummm . . ." said Luke. He didn't know why they were there either.

Just then, a very large, gray dog started to follow them. It was so big it looked like a wolf.

"Um, Father John?" said Becca nervously. "There's a wolf-dog getting close to us."

"Hello, Grigio!" said the priest happily to the dog. Then he turned to Luke, Becca, and Joshua. "This is Grigio. He's my friend."

"He looks scary," said Joshua.

The priest patted the dog on the head. Grigio's tail wagged, and his tongue hung out of his mouth. "He's here to keep me safe. Grigio protects me when I walk alone on dark streets."

"Where did he come from?" asked Becca.

"He's from God," Don Bosco said. "Sometimes my work takes me to unsafe neighborhoods. So God sends me Grigio to keep me safe. God always provides for what I need."

"Do you ever get scared?" asked Joshua.

"Sometimes," said Don Bosco. "But God keeps showing me, over and over, that He will take care of me. He is my Good Shepherd. He keeps me safe and gives me what I need."

Joshua started thinking about his new school again. He hung his head and looked at his shoes.

"What's the matter?" the priest asked Joshua.

"I was just thinking about school," said Joshua.

"Going to school is a great blessing," said Don Bosco.

Joshua kept looking at his shoes. "I'm scared," he said. "It's a new school. I don't know anyone there."

"Sounds like a great adventure to me!" said the priest. He smiled warmly at Joshua.

"But what if I don't fit in? What if I get lost? What if no one likes me?"

Don Bosco put his hand on Joshua's shoulder. "This sounds to me like you have a chance to show your trust in God."

"How?" asked Joshua.

"That is what true faith is," said Don Bosco. "It means believing in something that you can't prove. It means knowing God will take care of you even if you don't know for sure what will happen."

Joshua still wasn't sure. He didn't know what was going to happen at school tomorrow. "How do you know?" he asked.

"I know that God will provide for you. You have nothing to worry about," said Don Bosco.

They continued walking. Grigio walked behind them wagging his tail.

"I'm still not sure," said Joshua. He shrugged his shoulders.

"I'll have enough trust for both of us," said the priest. "Just like I know you have exactly eighteen cents in your pocket, I know God will take care of you."

Joshua reached into his pocket. He had one dime, one nickel, and three pennies. He had exactly eighteen cents. Joshua's eyes grew wide in amazement. He showed Luke and Becca the coins.

"How did you know that?" asked Luke. His mouth hung open in awe.

"You are a real magician," said Becca.

Father John Bosco smiled at the kids. "Trust me when I say that God will take care of you."

Joshua started to believe Don Bosco. He could tell that this was a man of God. If he believed, maybe Joshua could believe too.

They came to a gate. Behind it was a small house.

"This is my house," said the priest.

"Woof," said Grigio. The priest gave him one more pat on the head. The gray dog turned and started walking away. The kids blinked their eyes a few times. Grigio seemed to disappear as they were watching.

"Where did he go?" asked Joshua.

Don Bosco laughed a little bit. "Grigio comes and goes. When I need him, he'll be back."

"I think it's time for us to go too," said Joshua. He knew it was time to go back home. He was ready to go to his first day at the new school.

Chapter 7
Back Home Again

Don Bosco said goodbye to the kids. He walked through the gate to his house.

Once they were alone, Luke, Becca, and Joshua knew what to do. They would pray the Guardian Angel prayer. Then Rafael would know they were ready to go home.

They prayed together: "Angel of God, my guardian dear, to whom God's love commits me here. Ever this day, be at my side, to light and guard, to rule and guide. Amen."

They finished the prayer and opened their eyes. Rafael had

appeared. He floated in the air, shimmering brightly.

"Have you finished here?" the angel asked the children.

"Yes," said Joshua.

"We're ready to go home," said Becca.

Rafael smiled at them. "Wonderful," he said.

Rafael spread his arms wide. An image appeared before them. It looked like a movie screen had appeared out of nowhere. Instead of a movie on the screen, it was a picture of the boys' bedroom.

"Bye, Rafael," said Luke. He stepped through the screen into his bedroom.

"See you next time! Thank you!" said Becca. She and Joshua joined

Luke. Just like that, the street, the gate, and the angel were gone.

The kids turned in a circle, but all they saw was the boys' bedroom. They were back home.

"Kids!" yelled mom from down the hall. "Bedtime!"

"I better get to my room!" said Becca. She picked up her Bible from the ground. She waved as she left the room.

The boys went to the bathroom to brush their teeth. Then they went back to their room. They each checked their new outfit and put on their PJs.

Joshua and Luke climbed into their beds. Luke asked, "Are you feeling better about tomorrow?"

"I am," replied Joshua. "I still don't know what's going to happen.

But I do know that God will be with me. He will take care of me."

"Exactly," said Luke.

"Saint John Bosco is really cool," said Joshua. "I still don't know how he knew how much money I had."

"For sure," said Luke. "He is the most talented priest I've ever met."

The bedroom door opened, and Mom and Dad came in.

"We came to say goodnight," said Dad.

"Are you both feeling okay about school?" asked Mom.

"Yes," said Luke.

"I am now," said Joshua.

"Starting a new school can be scary," said Dad.

"I know God will be with me," said Joshua. "He will provide for me, even if I don't know what's going to happen."

"That's right," said Mom. "I'm so glad you know that."

Joshua smiled at his parents. "I only just learned this from Saint John Bosco."

"The patron saint of schoolchildren!" said Mom. "What a great model and example of the faith."

"Could we include Saint John Bosco in our prayers tonight?" asked Joshua.

"Of course," said Dad. "Let's pray. In the name of the Father, and of the Son, and of the Holy Spirit. Amen. Lord, thank You for today. Thank You for our family. Be with the kids as they start a new school year tomorrow."

Dad squeezed Mom's hand. She continued, "Bless us, especially Joshua on his first day. Saint John Bosco, pray for us."

"Amen," they all said together.

Mom and Dad gave them each a kiss and left the room. Luke and Joshua lay in the dark.

"Night, Joshua," said Luke. His voice was sleepy. He would be asleep soon.

"Night," Joshua said back. He still felt a little nervous about tomorrow. He kept reminding himself about Grigio and that God always provided. He closed his eyes and thought of all his blessings.

He thought about his mom and dad. He thought about Becca and Luke. He thanked God for his family. Joshua thought about his new outfit for school. He thanked God for the clothes he had. He thought about the water balloon fight and the fun he had with his family.

Joshua didn't exactly remember how, but he fell asleep.

Chapter 8
The First Day of School

Joshua heard the bedroom door creak open. Mom's voice sang quietly, "Oh, rise and shine, and give God your glory, glory."

Joshua smiled. It was the first day of school. He still felt a little nervous, but he knew it would be okay.

The boys got up and dressed in their new clothes. They liked having a new outfit for a new school year. They each had a bowl of cereal for breakfast.

Becca, Luke, and Joshua got in Mom's car for the quick drive to school. Joshua felt the butterflies in his stomach grow. The closer he got to school, the less sure he felt.

They pulled into the parking lot. Joshua didn't want to get out of the car. Once he did, he would be alone. Luke would go to the 5th grade hall. Becca would go to the 3rd grade hall. He had to go to the 2nd grade hall alone.

Joshua forced himself to say bye to Mom. He stepped out of the car. He looked around. There were so many kids. He didn't know anyone.

He walked inside and started toward the 2nd grade hallway. He looked down as he walked.

"Hi," said a friendly voice. Joshua thought it was meant for someone else. He just kept walking.

"Are you new here?" asked the same voice.

This time Joshua looked up. There was a boy looking at him.

"Me?" asked Joshua. Was he talking to Joshua?

"Yeah," said the other boy. "I haven't seen you before."

"I am new," said Joshua. "Today's my first day."

"Cool," said the boy. "I'm Nathan. What's your name?"

"I'm Joshua," he replied.

"Are you in 2nd grade?" asked Nathan.

"Yes," said Joshua. "Are you?"

"I am," said Nathan. Both boys were smiling now. Nathan asked, "Who's your teacher?"

"Ms. Harken," replied Joshua.

"Me too!" said Nathan. "We can walk together."

Joshua felt so happy. The boys walked together and talked. Nathan told Joshua he has one sister. She is only two, so Nathan loves school. He likes to have kids his own age to play with.

Nathan showed Joshua the way to Ms. Harken's room. They walked past the cafeteria where Joshua would eat lunch.

Nathan showed him the school library. It was full of so many books.

Nathan even pointed out the bathroom on the way. Nathan knew where everything was.

"I can stay with you today so you don't get lost," said Nathan.

"Thank you," Joshua said. He felt so grateful for Nathan. Just like that, he knew he wouldn't get lost on his first day.

They arrived at Ms. Harken's room. "Here's our room," said Nathan. He turned to face Joshua.

Joshua looked down at Nathan's shirt. He was wearing a gray T-shirt. There was a wolf on it. Joshua smiled. The shirt reminded him of Grigio. Just like for Saint John Bosco, God had sent a gray wolf to help him.

Joshua felt happy as he walked into the classroom. "Do you like wolves?" he asked Nathan.

"I do," said Nathan. "Did you know they're related to dogs?"

"Yeah," said Joshua. "They can be very loyal and protective." Joshua thought about how loyal Grigio was. John Bosco was lucky to have him.

The boys put their backpacks in the cubbies. They took out their lunches and put them in the lunch bin. Even though this was a new school, it was a lot like Joshua's old school.

Joshua saw a big whiteboard. There were bookshelves with lots of books. He was looking forward to reading some of them. Ms. Harken had a lot of colorful posters on the walls. The classroom looked like fun.

The two boys looked around for their desks. They found their seats. They were sitting right next to each other.

"I wish I had a pet wolf," said Nathan. "My mom said no way. But I think it would be cool."

"I know someone who had a pet dog that looked like a wolf," said Joshua.

"You do?" asked Nathan.

"Yeah," said Joshua. "Have you ever heard of John Bosco?"

"No," said Nathan. "Who's that?"

Just like that, a friendship started. Joshua knew God was looking out for him. Joshua had a good feeling. It was going to be a great year.

The End

About Saint John Bosco

Saint John Bosco lived in the 1800s in Italy. His father died when he was two, and his family was very poor. When he was a kid, a traveling circus came to town. John Bosco taught himself some of the tricks. Then he would entertain other children, and afterward, he would recite prayers or teach about God.

He always wanted to be a priest. Don Bosco dedicated his life to working with the teenage boys of

Turin. They were poor and didn't have much education. John Bosco opened a school to teach the boys skills so they could make money for their families. But he always included a magic show or a performance to keep the kids entertained.

Don Bosco understood the importance of having fun while learning. He also started a system of positive discipline. This means that he would reward the boys who made good choices instead of punishing those who made bad choices. This helped them want to make good choices.

Grigio was real, too! John Bosco called him his guardian angel. Grigio never ate. He would appear and disappear whenever John Bosco was in an unsafe area. There were even a few times when Grigio had to defend John Bosco.

John Bosco started a group called the Salesians of Don Bosco that is still active today. As of 2021, there are over 14,000 members. His methods still have a lasting impact.

John Bosco is the patron saint of all schoolchildren, editors, publishers, and stage magicians. His feast day is January 31.

Saint John Bosco, pray for us!

About the Author

 Maria Riley is a passionate Catholic author and editor who loves writing stories to teach the faith in simple and engaging ways. She is inspired by Jesus' example of teaching in parables, and her books similarly tell a story and share a message at the same time. You will find her volunteering with her parish when she's not writing or mom-ing around with her four daughters.

Maria lives in Kansas with her family, where they love reading, playing board games, and spending time exploring outside.

You can find Maria on Instagram and Facebook @MariaRileyAuthor.

About the Illustrator

 Emily Mae is an illustrator and author with two self-published children's books and who dreams of writing a young adult fantasy series. In 2022, she founded Kingdom Come Co., a Christian company that sells products for kids. She is also a certified organization specialist and owns an organizing company.

Emily lives in Connecticut with her family and enjoys drawing, reading, watching movies, homeschooling, crafting, praying, perusing Hobby Lobby, or following a creative passion.

You can find Emily's artwork on Instagram @emilymaecreates.

Adventures with the Saints

Go on more adventures
with Luke, Becca, and Joshua!

Adventures with the Saints #1
Saint Joseph: The Foster-Father Saint

Adventures with the Saints #2
Saint Thérèse: The Sleeping Saint

. . . With more to come!

Keep in Touch!

Visit www.MariaRileyAuthor.com to connect with me, get updates, and explore my other writing. Be among the first to know about what's new, plus order personalized autographed copies of all my books.

I love getting notes from readers! Ask Mom and Dad first, then email me at Maria@MariaRileyAuthor.com.

I can't wait to hear from you!

MARIA RILEY
AUTHOR

Made in United States
North Haven, CT
23 October 2024

59345961R00050